Sacral

Dance

Imagination

Silly

Colorful

Fun

Flow

Water

Magic

Joy

Creativity

Svadhisthana

Art

Play

Laughter

Orange

Sacral Chakra Adventures:

Dancing
with
Orange and Citrine

Volume 2

By: K.C. Gold

"This book is dedicated to you.
Your visions will shape your future."

Northern Lights Publishing LLC.

https://northernlightskids.com/

Orange and Citrine,
What a radiant pair we are,
We are spinning energy particles,
Where being creative makes us stars.

We reside within you
Where your creativity's the key,
Located around your lower belly,

Sacral Chakra, our name,
Where creativity brews,
Guiding your inspirations in
all that you choose.

But if you find your creativity waning,

Or
your emotions
starting to stew,

It's a sign we're unbalanced, needing help from you.

To spin back around,

417 times plus two,

Here are some suggestions

from us to you:

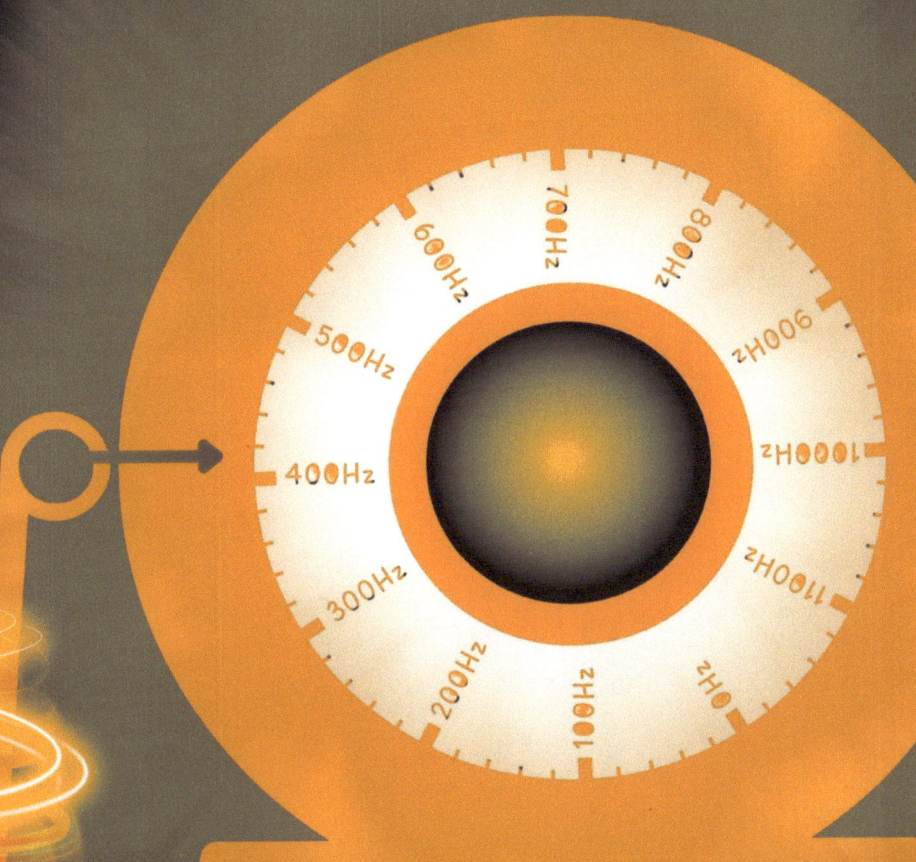

Hertz Meter

1 Hertz (Hz) = 1 Spin Per Second

417Hz

Sound gives our scenes a spark,
Note 'D' ignites us bright,
With its melody so sharp,
We will soar into the light.

In your tummy is a wheel of orange hue,
Where creativity dances and paints your sky anew.

Feast on orange fruits from nature's fertile mound,
Feel their vibrant energy dancing through you now.

Dress in shades
of orange's warmest glow,
Surround yourself
until you feel right at home.

In a quiet place,
let calmness hug you,
And when it does,
choose a mantra that feels
right for you.

"I am as creative as an artist at play; Colors swirl and dance in my mind every day."

"Ideas swirl in my playful head, Turning ordinary moments into adventures instead."

"I am creative like the flowing sea; Waves of ideas flow through me."

"Spreading smiles like confetti in the air, With joy as my currency, I'm a millionaire."

Let your creativity shine, let it set you free,
With Orange and Citrine, your true self you'll see.

With laughter and joy, let
your imagination play,
Sacral Chakra's magic will
light up your day.

Magic

Joy

Creativity

Art

Svadhisthana

Play

Laughter

Orange

Dear Reader,

Thank you for taking the time to read this book. If you found value in it, I would be incredibly grateful if you could take a few moments to leave a review. Your feedback not only helps me improve but also aids other readers in discovering books they might enjoy.

Thank you once again for your support and for being a part of this adventure!

Warm regards,
K.C. Gold

Amazon

Northern Lights Publishing

Your visions will shape your future.

www.ingramcontent.com/pod-product-compliance
Lightning Source LLC
Chambersburg PA
CBHW041434120626
46547CB00002B/212